KENN BIVINS

39 LESSONS FOR BLACK BOYS & GIRLS

KENN BIVINS

39 LESSONS FOR BLACK BOYS & GIRLS

INVISIBLE ENNK PRESS · ATLANTA

All inquiries received at:
Invisible Ennk Press
P.O. Box 69
Avondale Estates, GA 30002

First printing, 2020. Published by Invisible Ennk Press.

paperback **ISBN: 978-1-7333747-7-4**
ebook **ISBN: 978-1-7333747-8-1**

Design by Kenn Bivins.

for boys and girls
of all shades of Black

Being Black isn't a trend or a sin.
It's the skin and the lessons within.

– Kenn Bivins

First of all, why is this book necessary? Isn't the title somewhat divisive? What does this book have to say that the previous ones in the 39 Lessons series didn't already say? This book is about race – specifically the Black race.

Being Black in the United States, or anywhere else for that matter, is a nuanced experience. It is within those layers, if left unaddressed, that identity can be lost.
So we must talk to our Black children about race.
If it's treated as a taboo topic, imagine how powerless and unloved Black children may eventually feel.

This book contains brief contextual use of the N-word and the B-word. These words are not used gratuitously

or frivolously. There is a likelihood our children have been exposed to these ugly words - or worse - have been addressed as such. It is up to us as parents, mentors, guardians, and the like to contextualize these two words and have a conversation with our children.

Thank you for reading.

love and power forever,
Kenn Bivins

01

YOUR BLACK IS BEAUTIFUL.

Your melanin, strength, creativity, versatility, faith, tenacity and intuition make you inherently beautiful.

02

YOUR SKIN DOES NOT MAKE YOU...

an n-word, a b-word, suspect, villain, thug, criminal, brute, slut, freak, or any negative thing. Your skin is instead the wrapper to all of the good things within.

03

YOU CAN'T BE A KING AND A N-WORD.

The bloodied, oppressive *n-word* can't be saved and ushered into camaraderie. Abandon using it to refer to your people. Instead, think and speak greater destinies about yourself and your loved ones.

04

YOU CAN'T BE A QUEEN AND A B-WORD.

A b-word is a female dog, or a person or thing that is very difficult. It is usually leveraged as an insult against a woman or a person perceived to be weak and inferior. You are greater than those things. Hold your head higher that they might see your crown.

05

THERE IS SO MUCH MORE TO YOUR HISTORY THAN SLAVERY.

We have contributed to innovations, science, literature, art and customs that have helped shape the culture of the United States and the world. Despite slavery, we found ways to survive and thrive beyond.

06

MINDSET IS YOUR SUPERPOWER.

Persistence, hard work and effort are all very important traits to have, but having that foundational belief that you are in control of your own destiny is the secret sauce to your success.

07

YOU ARE NOT A MINORITY.

Black people's cultural influence on the mainstream alongside their economic power and innovation has long established them as the foundation to mankind. And logically, people who are of the global majority can't be considered minorities.

08

THE WAY THEY SEE YOU SHOULD NEVER TAINT THE WAY YOU SEE YOURSELF.

You can't control what others think about you, but you can command what you think of yourself.

09

YOUR LIFE MATTERS.

Ignore the subtle diminishing of your value in the media, in the justice system, in education and in white-washed history. You are good enough.

10

READ A BOOK.
READ MANY BOOKS.

Reading books increases knowledge, reduces stress, expands vocabulary, builds analytical skills, improves memory, focus and writing skills, and is a great form of entertainment.

11

STUDY. PRACTICE. REPEAT.

There is no glory in practice,
but without practice there is no glory.

12

COLUMBUS DAY, THANKSGIVING, EMANCIPATION PROCLAMATION, ETC.

White-wash: to alter something in a way that favors, features or caters to White people, such as increasing their prominence, relevance or impact while minimizing or misrepresenting that of non-White people.

13

JUNETEENTH IS...

the June 19th celebration of the real liberation from slavery that came two and a half years after the Emancipation Proclamation was issued on January 1, 1863. 250,000 slaves in Texas were already free – but none of them knew it and no one was in a hurry to tell them.

14

MARCUS GARVEY,
PRIDE AND INNOVATION

He was a writer, gifted speaker and activist who established a corporation that offered stock for Black people to buy. The project generated income and provided jobs. There were numerous enterprises, including a chain of grocery stores and restaurants, a steam laundry, tailor shops, a publishing house and a doll factory.

15

IDA B. WELLS,
COURAGE AND EMPATHY

She was an unsung American hero, a journalist and an activist who investigated and reported lynchings all the way to the White House, calling for reforms. She was described as a woman with plenty of nerve who was as smart as a steel trap. She also fought for Black women's rights long before it was popular or safe.

16

KATHERINE JOHNSON,

GENIUS AND PERSEVERANCE

She was the mathematician who hand-calculated the trajectory for America's first trip to space. Despite segregation and discrimination, her calculations would be critical to the success of NASA's crewed space flights.

17

ELLEN AND WILLIAM CRAFT,

CUNNING AND RESOURCEFUL

The Crafts were a married couple who wanted to start a family so they escaped slavery by hiding in plain sight. Ellen resembled a White woman, so she cross-dressed as a male plantation owner, with William posing as her slave. They fled Georgia and lived in England for 19 years before returning to the United States and establishing a farm.

18

RACISM IS ALIVE AND WELL IN AMERICA.

When Barack Obama was elected the first Black president, racism didn't suddenly die. It simply evolved to thrive publicly in the form of legislation and policies that meshed bigoted ideologies with white-washed ignorance.

19

YOU DON'T HAVE THE SAME PRIVILEGE AS YOUR WHITE FRIENDS.

They're much less likely to be profiled by police, followed in a store, held accountable for others in their community, marginalized or judged according to the color of their skin. Be vigilant.

20

THEY ARE NOT BETTER THAN YOU. YOU ARE NOT BETTER THAN THEM.

Don't be an entitled human or support entitled humans.

21

YOU BELONG TO THE AFRICAN DIASPORA.

Diaspora means the dispersion of people from their homeland or community. As a Black person, you are a part of the African diaspora because your ancestors were dispersed from the continent of Africa to parts all over the world because of the slave trade and colonization.

22

ALL LAWS ARE NOT JUST.

People who enact laws are empowered by widespread voter ignorance and by strong biases of their own. It was said by one of the founding fathers of the United States that if a law is unjust, a man is not only right to disobey it, he is obligated to do so.

23

PROTEST IS THE RIGHT TO SPEAK AGAINST WHAT IS WRONG.

Don't let anyone shame you out of standing for what you believe is right. The United States was founded on protest.

24

EQUALITY AND EQUITY ARE NOT THE SAME.

You will win $500 if you can fly your paper plane farther than your classmates.
Equality supplies all of you with sheets of paper although some of them are crumpled up.
Equity makes sure that all of you have the same quality of paper to start with.

25

THEIR ICE WATER IS NOT COLDER THAN YOURS.

Corporations, restaurants and institutions don't sell a better product simply because they're White-owned. This belief is rooted in self-hate. Support Black business.

26

MAKE YOUR VOICE HEARD.

Be confident, ask questions, challenge authority and interact as an equal.

27

A RIOT IS THE LANGUAGE OF THE UNHEARD.

And what is it America has failed to hear? It has failed to hear that the promises of freedom and justice have not been met. And it has failed to hear that large segments of White society are more concerned about tranquility and the status quo than about justice and humanity.

- Martin Luther King Jr.

28

WE ARE NOT MONOLITHIC.

To be monolithic is to act and think the same.
We are not limited because of our "color."
We are individuals who are different
from one another in thought, beliefs,
practices and other characteristics.

29

CULTURAL APPROPRIATION IS...

the act of adopting (stealing) elements of another culture, including knowledge, practices and symbols, without understanding or respecting the original culture and context.

30

MICROAGGRESSION IS...

brief and commonplace daily verbal, behavioral or environmental indignities, whether intentional or unintentional, that communicate hostile, derogatory or negative racial slights and insults toward people of color.

31

LOOK THEM IN THE EYE.

It demonstrates confidence and trustworthiness, while acknowledging the value of the other person.

32

EXPLORE BEYOND YOUR DOOR.

Whether it's leaving your neighborhood, your city, your state or your country, aspire to travel.

33

MASTER THE ART OF CODE-SWITCHING.

Code-switching is the ability to modify one's language, dialects, styles, registers and behavior to adapt to different cultural environments. It is an extremely valuable skill in almost any career.

34

TRUST YOUR GUT.

Guts. You've had them since you were born. Trust them.

35

DON'T MARGINALIZE YOURSELF WITH LABELS.

And don't allow others to do it, either. It's a form of control that can limit your full potential.

36

BE CONSCIOUS, AWAKE AND AWARE.

Be vigilant of racism in society and other forms of oppression and injustice.

31

TAKE.

Take advice, seek assistance, be curious and graciously receive praise.

38

GIVE.

Give back, provide assistance, offer resources and grant acclaim.

39

SEEK GOD ALWAYS.

Whether you know God or not, continually seek answers. You are the dream. Discover the dreamer.

With the other books in the 39 Lessons series, I coined the phrase "love and laughter forever," but you've probably noticed that's not the case with this one.

On the following pages I explain why "love and power forever" was more important to emphasize in this book.

LOVE

It is important to be loved and reminded of love by constant affirmations and actions. Unfortunately, the world our Black children go into every day conspires to tell them they are unlovable.

All children (that means you) are worthy of love, respect and consideration. Whether the world acknowledges it or not, our Black children must still love themselves. Love is a verb.

POWER

Laughter should be synonymous with childhood,
but that's not a reality for many Black children.
Some of them are in conditions and environments where
they feel powerless, unheard and invisible.

When I was a child, I fantasized about having
superpowers so I could defeat the odds against me and
rescue others in need. Time revealed that I didn't need
superpowers to be empowered. I had my presence,
my resilience, my voice and a sense of self-esteem.
A raised fist became like Superman's cape.

FOREVER

The ankh was used in Egyptian hieroglyphics and art to represent the word for "life" or the "key of life."

The ankh is more appropriate than the previously utilized star, considering the subject matter and the audience. Love and power should be asserted and internalized without ceasing. Forever.

THE SIGNIFICANCE OF 39

You may be wondering, "What's the deal with 39? Why wasn't this book called 101 Lessons or something like that? 39 is just odd."

Well, let me explain. Years ago when I was blogging regularly, I went through what I lovingly regard as my "list phase." Lists are an amazing way to quantify accomplishments, goals, things to do, groceries, etc.

I ran across an internet challenge to detail random things about myself and this turned into a post titled "99 Things." This was my inaugural list, but it got so much feedback that I challenged myself further to write another list and then another, each one being

a quantity divisible by 3 and ending in 9. Apparently, I was also into numeric themes.

Fun fact: June is my favorite month. It's a reflective time because so many events happen that month that are significant to me. Father's Day, being among those events, prompted me to write a list from a dad's perspective. My numbering pattern had landed on 39 around the time this list was conjured and thus was born ***39 Lessons for Boys.***

Numerology indicates that 39 is associated with direction and guidance in discovering life's purpose. While I didn't know this at the time of the original writing, it's kismet how that worked out.

It's amazing to me how what seems so random can actually have meaning after all. So there you have it – the significance of 39.

love and power forever,
kenn

ADVICE FOR THE PARENTS OF BLACK BOYS & GIRLS

Parents, let's admit it: The rules are different for our Black babies. This system hasn't failed them. This system wasn't built for them. It can be quite daunting to bring them up in an environment that is prone to hostility toward them, but all is not lost.

You can raise Black boys who are elated and full of joy, and Black girls who are confident and love themselves. While it is revolutionary to be Black, happy and unbothered in this country, it is possible.

The following tips are guides toward that progressive end.

1. TALK TO THEM ABOUT THE POLICE.

Manage a healthy and safe perspective of the police.

2. ASK, THEN LISTEN.

Ask them open-ended questions, as if you are the one learning. Listen intently to their answers.

3. ANSWER QUESTIONS.

Feed their curiosity about all things trivial and difficult, all the while building their trust.

4. TAKE A BREAK.

Don't teach them that life is solely about work. Teach them the concept of self-care along the way.

5. HAVE FAITH.

Demonstrate an active belief and faith in God.

6. EAT GOOD.

Serve and eat food that is healthy for mind and body.

7. SHARE YOUR STORY.

Tell who you were as a child so they can learn more about where and who they come from.

8. SHOW THEM THE MONEY.

Teach them about saving and investing.

9. PLAY OUTSIDE.

Spend time playing with them in the fresh air and sunshine.

10. TAKE THEM ON VACATION.

Get away together to relax and recharge.

11. READ TOGETHER.

Connect through books (like this one).

WHO IS KENN BIVINS?

Kenn Bivins isn't an African-American studies professor at a prestigious institution nor does he hold a Ph.D. in child psychology. But he is a dad, uncle and mentor who knows what it's like to grow up in Black skin. It is from those experiences that ***39 Lessons for Black Boys & Girls*** was born.

Kenn is an illustrator turned author who has an affinity toward telling both heart-warming and heart-wrenching tales of redemption. Through his novels and nonfiction, he aspires for his readers to identify with the characters and themes that he crafts through suspense, intrigue, action and the unexpected.

His love of literature was born from reading comic books and honed by enjoying the works of Richard Wright, Ralph Ellison and John Steinbeck, among many.

His novels, ***the Wedding & Disaster of Felona Mabel*** and ***Pious***, have received much critical acclaim from the literary world.

Thank you for taking the time to read and consider this very important book. It's meant to be read multiple times and shared with others. And by share, I mean tell people where and how to get their own copy or gift them one. Just between you and me, I've learned not to loan books because I never get them back ☺

39 Lessons for Boys, ***39 Lessons for Girls*** and ***39 Lessons for Teens*** are also available. They make great companions to this book and look great together on a bookshelf or coffee table.

love and power forever,
Kenn Bivins

OTHER BOOKS BY KENN BIVINS

39 LESSONS FOR BOYS

39 LESSONS FOR GIRLS

39 LESSONS FOR TEENS

THE WEDDING & DISASTER OF FELONA MABEL

PIOUS

Made in United States
North Haven, CT
02 April 2022

17739364R00070